Understanding a Church:

what do you see and what does it mean?

by
Steven J. Schloeder

All booklets are published thanks to the generous support of the members of the Catholic Truth Society

CATHOLIC TRUTH SOCIETY
PUBLISHERS TO THE HOLY SEE

Contents

ISBN 978 1 86082 922 2

Introduction

In the middle of the twentieth century, there was a popular but curious notion that the church building itself really didn't matter, that the building was just a "skin for the liturgical action."[1] All that really mattered were the people gathered inside. However, we can demonstrate that church buildings themselves do mean something of considerable importance to the Catholic faithful. The church is not merely a container for the liturgical assembly to keep out the rain and snow, but the building is intended to help us understand both the liturgy and our place in the Church. The very forms and arrangements of the church building hold meaning for us: Catholic church buildings *mean* something, they are *designed* with *intention* to communicate meaning. Furthermore, there is a well-formed and consistent language to communicate a particular message.

The language of church architecture is the language of revelation, the same sorts of words, vocabulary, syntax, and grammar God uses to communicate something about himself. Throughout Scripture we read of God revealing himself to us: walking with Adam and Eve in the Garden,

---

[1] For instance, *Environment and Art in Catholic Worship*, Washington DC: United States Catholic Conference, 1978.

visiting Abram at the Oak of Mamre, appearing to Moses in the Burning Bush, leading Israel through the desert in the form of a pillar of fire, or being present among his people in the *Shekinah* - the "glory of the Lord" - in the Temple. In the fulness of time, God perfectly revealed himself to us in Jesus Christ, the Word incarnate.

This language of revelation forms the basis of our thinking about God, the Church, and the sacraments. It is necessarily a language of metaphor, analogy and symbol, since that is the only way the human mind can know the spiritual, non-material, and numinous. God speaks to us through a *sacramental* language, which constitutes the essential language structure of not only the seven sacraments, but of liturgy, revelation, architecture, art, and even the human person. Our human experience of the sacred is completely enmeshed in this sacramental language of liturgical forms and architectural meaning. The main purpose of church architecture is not the simple accommodation of a group of people to do something within - lots of buildings do that - but rather the church building is a way of understanding these relationships that are ultimately an expression of God's love relationship with humanity. At the most foundational level, the Church intends to express these relationships when building a church.

Architectural Sign Language

Our Catholic understanding of anthropology holds that the human being is both rational and social. *Social* in that we are made for relationships (we are made for God); *rational* in that we use reason to understand our existence and the order of creation. From these two first principles, we can better understand why God created us as symbol-knowing, symbol-making and symbol-using beings.

The bedrock of the Catholic faith is the Gospel message of God's love relationship with all of humanity. It is indeed *catholic*: universal, cross-cultural, and transgenerational. There is not one principle, message, or set of rules for the Christian and another for the non-Christian. The baptized believer shares exactly the same human nature as the unbaptised, save for the spiritual regeneration through the Sacrament of Baptism to become a son or daughter of God. Nothing changes for the Christian in the essential way that the soul operates. We still have a fallen human nature that imperfectly seeks to know the truth through the intellect. We all desire various goods through the will. We are all beset with all the human foibles of ego, vice, sin, and imperfection.

Christian or pagan, atheist or agnostic, we all live an intensely symbolic existence: everything we know about anything outside of our own self is understood through symbols, and this symbolic method of knowing is inherently relational and rational. This process is the core of our *rationality*: we learn of new things by making *ratios* (comparisons) between things that are somehow alike, and understand them as different things from those we already know, by understanding the relationships between them. When we learn of a new discrete thing or type, we give it a new name. We thus are assigning signs and symbols (for words are a type of symbol) to keep different things separated in our mind for clarity of thought and communication.

We only know God indirectly and imperfectly, mediated through God's direct revelation, but also mediated through our bodies and our senses, our minds and our hearts, words and symbols and gestures and patterns. Everything we know about God, or can say about God, is by analogy: to call God 'Father' or Jesus 'Lord' or to speak of the 'Kingdom of God' or say that 'God is love' is all based on symbolic analogies of what we know imperfectly about 'father', 'lord', 'kingdom', or 'love'. As Dorothy Sayers wrote,

> All language about God must, as Saint Thomas Aquinas pointed out, necessarily be analogical. We need not be surprised at this, still less suppose that because

it is analogical it is therefore valueless or without any relation to the truth. The fact is, that all language about everything is analogical; we think in a series of metaphors. We can explain nothing in terms of itself, but only in terms of other things. ...It may be perilous, as it must be inadequate, to interpret God by analogy with ourselves, but we are compelled to do so; we have no other means of interpreting anything.[2]

Certainly, all language, art, metaphor, ritual, advertising and poetry depend on the power of the symbol to communicate. Words themselves are symbols that encode a whole constellation of meaning, history, thoughts, emotions, and associations. So too the work of art, the symbol that is intended to invoke and elicit both a rational and emotional response - a fully human response.

So whereas Adam and Eve walked with God in the Garden, we only know and experience God through mediating symbols, through revealed images and through sacraments. Our first parents knew God as he is: directly, immediately, intimately; we only now know him in reference to other things: indirectly, mediated through symbols, by analogy to other things we understand. As St Paul tells us, "Now we are seeing a dim reflection in a mirror; but then we shall be seeing face to face." (*1 Co* 13:12)

---

[2] Dorothy Sayers. *The Mind of the Maker*, London: Methuen and Co. 1941. pp. 17-18.

Despite this condition of alienation from God after the Fall, God continued to communicate and express his relationship with us through signs, symbols and sacraments. This is one way of thinking about salvation history: how after the Fall, God revealed himself and communicated to us, and what that symbol language consisted of. All matters of theology, liturgy, and sacred architecture are necessarily concerned with this language that reveals God's intention, for all these are incomprehensible without understanding this language.

The Church Building as a Sacramental

Catholic church architecture strives to express this intention in the forms and arrangements of the building. The building itself is a *sacramental*, properly speaking: it is a material object which is permanently consecrated to be a means of grace for Christ's faithful. We should recall the difference between the seven sacraments, and the various *sacramentals* that the Church gives us. The seven sacraments are all instituted by Jesus himself as objective means of participating in the life of grace. Christ objectively acts to give us grace as we partake in the sacraments because they are part of his plan for our salvation as he has instructed the Church through the apostles. The sacraments don't just point to something of God, but they are the only way that we objectively participate in the life of God.

Sacramentals are similar to the sacraments, but they are instituted by the Church rather than by Christ himself. They are not objective occasions of grace, but rely very much on our subjective disposition: the Eucharist is Christ whether we believe or not, whether we want to receive or not. Conversely, a sacramental requires our active co-operation to receive the grace that the Church imparts as we

The church building is a sacramental: it is a sign and symbol of the heavenly realities.

engage in the occasion of grace. But like one of the seven sacraments, a sacramental always involves a perceptible thing that the Church has anointed or blessed to be the occasion of grace, like a blessed rosary or a scapular, or holy water or the Stations of the Cross, or even sacred time such as a feast day or the call to fast. Through the prayers of the Church the sacramentals prepare us to receive grace and to co-operate with grace: they are small ways in which we can grow in sanctification and in God's love.

A church building is a sacramental in this sense. The Church erects buildings for the most important thing the Church does, which is the worship of God and the sanctification of the people of God through the Holy Mass. Other important things also occur in these buildings of course: the other sacraments, devotional life, evangelisation, education and catechesis, community building and service; but the celebration of the Sacred Liturgy is the core reason for which a church is built. Like all the other sacramentals, the Church blesses the material object of the church building for the sanctification of the faithful and it is set aside, reserved, for the special purpose of sanctification. And like all the other sacramentals, the building itself, and the arrangement of the various parts thereof, has a formal language that is integral with how we use it.

This should make it clear why a church is more than "a skin for the liturgical action", and why thinking it no more than that does a massive disservice both to the Sacred Liturgy and to the people of God. We are both body and soul, and endowed with memory and imagination. We come to God in the fulness of our humanity, not just functionally "gathering together". Catholicism speaks to the fulness of our humanity, and the Church calls us through our mind and heart, will and intellect, memory and imagination, and our capacity for beauty. The Church always rightly asserts the goodness of the material world, and has always been supportive of the arts to convey the message of the Gospel, to move our hearts and draw us closer to God. If a church building fails to do this, it fails as a church. If it succeeds in this, if it supports the Holy Mass, if it elicits in us a sense of the holy, if it draws us into some foretaste of the divine beauty, then the building is well designed to serve its sacramental purpose.

On Seeing a Church

So let's walk up to a church. It doesn't really matter what city or town you are in, whether you are approaching a large urban cathedral or a small village parish church. The first question to ask - it seems kind of elementary, but it really isn't - is "how do you know it's a church?"

Is there something in the shape of the building, its composition or its materials, or the way it sets on the site that tells you it's an important building? Do you only know it's a church because there is a sign announcing "Queen of the Apostles" or "The Catholic Community of St James"? Is it mostly because there is a cross on the building, and if so, does anything else about the building suggest to you that you are approaching a significant building where something important occurs?

We ask this because in the language of architecture (and like all languages, architecture relies on its own grammar, context, metaphors and analogies, syntax and arrangement to communicate something) there are patterns by which we know a building is important or significant. These tend to be closely connected with the way the building is intended to function: large civic buildings such as the city hall, courts, libraries, and schools have more prominent places in the urban fabric than warehouses, apartment buildings or private offices.

In thinking about the way a church building presents itself to the city, the landscape, or the street, we can consider that by analogy we know individual people primarily by their faces. Do we intuitively sense what this building represents by its primary 'face' (its façade), which is the entrance and the main expression of the building? Does the church present a strong visage to us? Does it look us in the eye and announce its message clearly and evangelically? Or does it avert its eyes, shy away, and hide its intention among the jumble of other banal buildings in the urban fabric?

Again, is there a clear sense of entry, and therefore a sense of welcome? Or are we forced to wonder how to enter the building, unsure if we are going in the right door? Is there any sense of the individual parts making up a greater whole, as a human body is comprised of other parts making an organic unity? Does the building speak of the memory of the Church either through the arrangement of the architectural forms or some nod to the historical styles that have informed our cultural memory of what churches look like? Does it speak through the iconography and imagery of statuary, mosaics and other art about Christ, Our Lady, the angels and saints? Does it invoke some analogy of the Church such as the holy mountain, the body of Christ, the celestial city, or another scriptural image of the kingdom of God?

If we ask these questions as we approach a church building, we will start to see it in the way the Church wants us to see it: as a sacred place in which we can encounter God because God is coming towards us in the material world and inviting us into a closer spiritual relationship with him. The way this happens is the story of the timeless encounter of God with humanity, revealed both in the Old Testament and in the New Testament. As we now enter the church building, let us keep in mind those ideas.

On Entering a Church

By the time we reach the main doors of a traditional church we might be anticipating something special. Perhaps we have had to climb a set of stairs that give a sense of ascension: "Come, let us go up to the mountain of the Lord, to the Temple of the God of Jacob" (*Is* 2:3). There might be a large forecourt that we cross around which other buildings are grouped - rectory, administration, social hall, classrooms, and the like. This sort of intermediate space that we cross from the parking lot or the hustle-bustle of the city street is not only psychologically beneficial, as we leave behind secular cares and enter into a sacred reality, but can also be seen as a sort of "town plaza" in the heavenly city. Perhaps we are called to enter through a triumphal arch, an architectural device inherited from the Roman emperors, through which we are entering into the triumph of Christ's victory. Perhaps above the doors is a large and glorious *tympanum*, an arched artistic work in sculpted stone or mosaic, with a depiction of Christ in Glory announcing that this is truly the *domus Dei*, the House of God, where Christ reigns supreme.

The doors themselves might well be true works of art, like the famous bronze doors of St Denis that bid the pilgrim not to merely to be dazzled by the beauty of the doors but rather focus on the beauty of Christ who is the true door. Christ called himself "the sheep gate" and "the door" through which we enter into salvation (*Jn* 10:9), and from time immemorial Christians have understood the symbolic importance of the door as a portal between not only places, but realities: "Then, in my vision, I saw a door open in heaven." (*Rv* 4:1).

This is a deep intuition, and important to the religious consciousness. So for the Christian, the door to the church is a sacred passage into the body of Christ since Christ himself was the true door, as Augustine recalls, where we enter into the life of Christ by entering into his death.[3] A church's main door means more than just an entrance to a building; it is a symbol of a whole process of transition and conversion. This is culturally enshrined in the Church's venerable practice of opening the "Holy Doors" at the Vatican basilica during the Jubilee years promulgated by the Pope. Entering the church means leaving the world behind and entering the kingdom of God; it allows us to cast off workaday cares and troubles to find solace, healing, and sanctuary. It is even a foretaste of entering the very gates of heaven, in that "the earthly liturgy is a foretaste of the heavenly liturgy."[4]

---

[3] St Augustine, *Tractate* 45, 15..

[4] Vatican Council II, *Sacrosanctum Concilium*, no. 8 [=SC].

The church doors both unite and make distinct two aspects of reality: the spiritual and the material, the sacred and the secular, the heavenly and the earthly, the timeless and the chronological. We enter a church to be restored in our relationship with God through the sacraments, by which we are healed and strengthened as we worship the Lord. Likewise, we enter to be fed and nourished on his Body and Blood and instructed in the Word of God, as well as to be sustained though the relationships among the people of God. But this is not only for our own good - Catholicism is not merely a private and personal relationship with God but rather a corporate and social one as well, and we are given graces both for ourselves and for the world. Hence, the doors also call us back into the secular world, the social and political and relational realms, where we are called to bring the Gospel to our neighbours, to evangelise and to bring Christ's love to others. Indeed, we should enter to worship, and exit to serve - this is what a church door is all about.

The Vestibule or Narthex

As we enter into the church proper we may first enter into a vestibule, or a narthex, a rather functional room for getting out of the cold or heat, for displaying church notices, parish bulletins, bookracks, and for after-Mass refreshments and other social functions that properly belong outside the nave.

This was not always such a functionalist space. In the early Church, the vestibule was a place for those who could not participate at Mass. The *disciplina arcani* was the ancient practice where only baptised Christians could be present at Mass. In the symbolic thought of the Church Fathers the vestibule was considered part of the unredeemed world, where the nave was the redeemed world and the sanctuary was heaven itself. So it was that pagans and catechumens, as well as the excommunicated and the penitents were relegated to the vestibule, with the deacons as door keepers to maintain the practice. Here in the vestibule those not admitted to Communion could hear the Gospel and the instructions without participating in the Eucharistic mysteries.

Today, the vestibule serves basic necessary functions we noted above: it's basically a covered area to get out of the elements. It is not part of the consecrated realm of the church building, but rather a functional and somewhat utilitarian space that is supportive of, but secondary to, the liturgical and devotional needs of the parish or cathedral. That said, the vestibule also often serves as an assembly area for liturgical processions and bridal parties, as well as a place for the parish priest to greet the faithful after Mass, and hence is sometimes popularly called a "gathering space". In the older form of the baptismal rite (as we shall see) the candidates are greeted at the entrance to the church, typically in this vestibule. Similarly, in the funeral rite, the gathered faithful and body of the deceased are greeted at the main entrance of the church where the body is blessed in remembrance of baptism.

But even while serving those other utilitarian functions, the vestibule is also a sort of transitional space between from the secular to the sacred. Mircea Eliade writes of this process in his discussion of the difference between sacred and profane spaces:

> For a believer, the church shares in a different space from the street in which it stands. The door that opens on the interior of a church actually signifies a solution of continuity. The threshold that separates the two spaces also indicates the distance between the two modes of being, the profane and the religious. The threshold is the limit, the boundary, the frontier that distinguishes

and opposes two worlds - and at the same time the paradoxical place where those worlds communicate, where passage from the profane to the sacred world becomes possible.[5]

So the vestibule is one stage of the threshold process, whereby we pass from our cars or the pavement, through the forecourt and into the vestibule before entering into the nave on the path to the altar.

[5] Mircea Eliade, *The Sacred and the Profane: The Nature of Religion*, trans. Willard R. Trask (New York: Harcourt, Brace, 1959), p. 25.

The baptistery at Saint Clare of Assisi alludes to the ancient octagonal form, yet opens up to the view of the entire nave. The raised infant font and the draining floor allow for a variety of methods for celebrating the sacrament.

The Baptistery

When we enter a church we reach for the holy water stoup to bless ourselves, in a symbolic renewal of our baptismal vows. By baptism we enter the Church, and so baptism is the first sacrament. So, while the door is the proper entrance into the house of God, both in the sense that Christ is the door (*Jn* 10:9) and Revelation shows us that the door to heaven leads us to the heavenly liturgy (*Rv* 4:1), our consideration of the baptismal font might well have preceded the discussion about the doors.

This act of blessing ourselves is part of our entering into the weekly (or daily) Mass, which itself is a compression of the yearly liturgical cycle.

We might start by understanding that the holy water stoup receives its symbolic imagery from the baptismal font, but the font receives its imagery from creation itself. Water and the Spirit, the formless and the active power of God that gives form to all things, are among the most primal elements of sacramental symbolism, preceding even "light" and "earth". As the Second Epistle of Peter tells us, "there were heavens at the beginning stood there, and that the earth was formed by the word of God out of water and between the waters" (*2 P* 3:5). The Spirit and water are so primal that Christ commands, "Unless a man is born through water and the Spirit, he cannot enter the kingdom of God" (*Jn* 3:5). And thus Christ began his own ministry through the baptism of John the Baptist, when the Holy Spirit came upon him in the form of a dove (*Mt* 3:16-17). This parallelism is most deliberate: as God first ordered the cosmos with water and the Spirit, and prepared the earth to receive humanity, so Christ restores that relationship both cosmically and in the soul of each Christian who is likewise brought into the kingdom through both water and the Spirit.

In the Genesis account of creation and the Garden, there were no doors or portals or gates or walls. The gates of paradise could only be said to be closed after the expulsion; before that all of creation was the domain of man as part of the "garden of delight" into which God placed Adam and Eve. Doors, gates, portals, and such (along with all the symbolism of dwelling apart from nature: the cave, the tent, the house, the temple) are consequences of alienation from God. Yet in the heavenly Jerusalem Christ himself is the gate, and he calls all nations to himself (*Rv* 21:26).

Thus baptism not only commences our journey in Christ, it also both causes us to participate in his Passion, death, and resurrection, and is a foretaste and promise of our destination in Christ. As St Justin Martyr tells us of the primitive Christian practice, the catechumens to be baptised are first brought to a place where there is water, and after the new Christian has been washed is then brought to the places of the Eucharistic assembly.[6] Not until the *neophyte* (literally, 'new planting' as part of the vine and branches imagery) was received into the Church and taught the fuller mysteries of the Faith, would he or she be admitted to the Eucharist.

The place of baptism in the primitive Church could be any place with water: a public bath, a town well, a spring or river or lake or sea.

However, at some early point, perhaps due to the decorum needed for the nude baptisms, as well as for the general sense of the solemnity of the rite, the early Church set aside special places for baptism. The earliest known surviving example is found in the ancient house-church at Dura Europos (c. AD 232), where a special room off the central courtyard, set apart from the main liturgical area, was converted to an elaborately decorated baptistery.

Soon after Christianity was made legal by Constantine (AD 313), and the Christian population rapidly grew, the Church started erecting free-standing baptisteries to accommodate the sacrament. These were often octagonal in specific recollection of the eighth day on which Christ rose from the dead - St Ambrose among others draws out this architectural parallel in a late fourth century epigram:

The octagon is raised for a sacred purpose
For which the octagonal font is also worthy

---

[6] Justin Martyr, *First Apology*, 61 and 65.

For this number eight aptly signs the sacred baptistery
In which the people are raised to true health restored
By the light of the Risen Christ who unlocks the gates
Of death and raises the dead from the grave.[7]

These ancient baptisteries were rich in scriptural allusion, architectural form, and ritual function, and were opportunities for great artistry and expression. The octagon was not only a mausoleum form, but a site memorial, a sort of martyrion that commemorated the location of the River Jordan where Christ was baptised. In addition to the widely used octagonal form, baptisteries and fonts could be cruciform, hexagonal, simple bowls, trefoils, or reused funereal sarcophaguses.

The baptism rite is a sacramental restoration of the alienated relationship between God and humanity, expressed in a highly compressed and complex language of ritual and symbol. It takes its symbolic cues from the Genesis account of creation, the Spirit of God hovering over the waters, and from the notion of the return to the Garden that is the eschatological fulfilment of salvation history. In baptism we are restored to our relationship with God, brought into the community of the Church,

---

[7] *Octachorum santos templum surrexit in usus / octagonus fons est munere dignus eo / hoc numero decuit sacri baptimatis aulam / surgere quo populus vera salus rediit / luce resurgentis Christi qui claustra resolvit / mortis et e tumulis suscitat exanimes*. The Latin is complex and subtle, and can admit of many emphases in translation.

participate in the Passion, death, and resurrection of Christ, are washed clean of our sins, claimed from the kingdom of the Satan for the kingdom of God, and sealed with the Blood of the Lamb that allows us entrance into the gates of the heavenly Jerusalem

This is well put in the older form of baptism (the Roman Ritual of 1962) wherein this process of passage from the kingdom of darkness to the kingdom of Christ is expressed through the symbols of doors, gates, illumination, and the waters of baptism: each a sort of threshold experience. The gates of the baptistery tell the parents that baptism is a 'rite of passage' in the deep sense of transitioning from one status to another: from the slaves of sin to sons and daughters of God; from "poor, banished children of Eve" to those whose names are written in the book of Life. The gates symbolise the recovery of Adamic innocence in Christ that allows us to enter into the ever-open gates of the heavenly Jerusalem and once again eat of the tree of Life. Indeed, Ghiberti's famous doors at the Baptistery in Florence were aptly named by Michelangelo as "the gates of Paradise", as baptism allows us to enter into the heavenly Jerusalem through the door, the sheep gate, that is Christ.

So as we continue our entrance into the church, look for the font. What messages are being communicated? Is it tucked in a dark corner, behind an imposing metal gate? Or is it a grand symbolic gesture that is in full view of the nave? Is it a simple infant font on a pedestal, or does it look like a large spa, perhaps with trickling water expressive of "streams of living water"? Does it speak of the various complexities of baptism: womb and tomb, welcome, washing, nourishment, death and resurrection, origin and culmination of salvation history? Or is its message more univalent: a simple "welcome, use this water to bless yourself since we don't have holy water stoups"?

The baptistery, of course, can assume many different forms and expressions, and be located in a number of different areas in the church. Each possible placement reflects some of the various, multivalent symbols encoded in the rite of baptism.

The Nave

We now pass into the body of the church, the *nave* as it is called, where the congregation is typically seated in pews. We are often taught that the nave takes its name from the idea of a ship - the Latin *navis*, whence comes 'navy' and 'navigate'. Indeed, in many churches the nave seems to be a sort of great upturned boat hull, especially if the ceiling is an exposed wooden roof like the ribbing and planks of a ship. There is also a linguistic association with the Greek *naus* (the root of words like *nautical*, *astronaut*, and even *nausea* as "ship sickness"), and the idea of being in a great boat - Noah's Ark or the Barque of Peter - conjuring up the imagery that we are saved from the destruction of the floods or the Last Judgement only by being "on board".

Despite the obvious affinities of the Church to the Barque, and the church ceiling to an upturned hull, the term "nave" does not come directly from *navis* (ship) but rather from *naos*, the Greek word for a shrine or a temple. The *naos* was the inner shrine of the pagan temple, the place where the image of the deity was kept, akin to the Holy of the Holies in the Jewish Temple. The sense of "boat" is secondary, although there also seems to be a dim connection between the two Greek words *naos* and *naus*, from the common root *naio*, meaning "to dwell": the pagan god dwelt in the *naos*, the boat (*naus*) allows us to dwell on the sea. Both are sorts of containers for habitation, both allow us to survive and thrive in alien and hostile environments, whether on the seas or dry land. One can think of a boat as floating house, much as the house was a primitive temple for the family religion. These sorts of deep symbolic connections are largely lost to us today, but they constitute the essential grammar of our religious thinking. We tend to take them for granted and ignore them in the same way we ignore the individual letters that make up a word or the individual words that make up a sentence, yet without those individual letters or words we cannot think about anything at all.

In the Christian dispensation, not only are the pagan gods turned upside down and pitched from their dais, but the temple itself is turned inside out. As J. Rykwert notes, the pagan temple was a secret and occult place for the gods: the image of the deity was in a dark chamber only accessed by the priests, a pattern also delegated to Moses and Solomon in the ordering of the Tent of Dwelling and the Temple.[8] Only initiates could enter the space of the temple shrine for their votive offering, or entrust that duty to the temple priests. Conversely, the universal message of Christianity made for a truly civic religion, one that

---

[8] J. Rykwert, *Church Building*, London: Burns and Oates, 1966.

encompassed all men and women, one that destroyed all claims and obligations to specific deities and the myriad of cults that dotted the pagan religious landscape.

The nave therefore opens up the temple to admit the entire Body of Christ. The *naos*, that ancient term still used throughout Eastern Christianity, speaks of the place outside of the sanctuary where the laity gather for the Divine Liturgy. In adopting and adapting this word from the pagan usage, the Church expresses the great Christian innovation that all the baptised are now admitted to the inner sanctum, to witness for themselves and participate directly in the mysteries of the Faith. No longer were the idols of false gods hidden in dark places attended to by a select coterie of priests, no longer was the Levitical priesthood the mediator between God and man, but in Christ all were now called upon to offer their "living bodies as a holy sacrifice, truly pleasing to God" (*Rm* 12:1). This is the essential meaning of the nave, a place where the Body of Christ dwells in the people gathered in the divine worship of the liturgy.

In thinking about the metaphor of the church building as a human body (see my earlier CTS booklet *Catholic Architecture*[9]), the nave is basically the whole torso of the body. Where the sanctuary speaks of the "head" (Christ as the head of the Church), the nave speaks of the body:

---

[9] Schloeder, *Catholic Architecture*, London: Catholic Truth Society, 2013.

all the vital functions and parts needed for circulation, respiration and digestion. It is integrally related to, but separate and distinct from, the sanctuary (which we will discuss next) but operates as part of the one organic body. As St Maximus the Confessor wrote,

> In a church, the sanctuary and the nave communicate: the sanctuary enlightens and guides the nave, which becomes its visible expression. Such a relationship restores the normal order of the universe, which has been destroyed by the fall of man. Thus it re-establishes what had been in paradise and what will be in the Kingdom of God.[10]

Within this understanding, we can see parallels to what we considered in the cosmic imagery of baptism, a restoration of the divine plan in Christ writ large in the architectural forms of the church building. The narthex, or vestibule, the area for the penitents and catechumens, is the unredeemed world anticipating the Gospel of Jesus Christ. The nave is the redeemed world, and is an image of the perfection of creation. In the eastern Churches, this area is typically surmounted with a dome, recalling the heavens and "the new heavens and new earth" (*2 P* 3:13) with an image of Christ the Pantocrator. But the dome also suggests that the *naos* is the womb of the Virgin, as well as the holy cave of Bethlehem and the holy cave of the

---

[10] St. Maximus the Confessor, *Mystagogia*, 8.21.

Sepulchre. Thus it evokes many images of places where the Church is vivified by the Spirit, born into the world, and redeemed into the glory of the Lord.

This baptismal imagery is subtly expressed in the *Rite of Dedication of a Church*. One of the first acts the bishop does is to bless the water and to sprinkle the gathered faithful since it is the faithful who are the spiritual temple, built of living stones to receive the dwelling of the Holy Spirit. (*1 Co* 6:19; *1 P* 2:5). The bishop then sprinkles the walls of the nave, the material temple, as a sort of figure of baptism. In the middle ages, the bishop would circumambulate the church three times, sprinkling the walls with water, to represent the threefold immersion of baptism. Similarly, as the baptismal candidate is anointed with oils using the sign of the cross, so the walls of the nave are anointed in twelve places with oil on the consecration crosses, representing the twelve apostles. Such symbolism is quite deliberate, as the medieval theologian Hugh of Saint-Victor tells us:

> We must speak of the dedication of a church, just as of the first baptism by which the church itself in a manner is baptised, that in it after a fashion men may be baptised to be regenerated unto salvation. …Regeneration is first symbolised in the dedication of a church; then it is exhibited in the sanctification of a faithful soul.[11]

---

[11] Hugh of Saint-Victor, *De Sacramentis*, bk. 2, pt. 5, 1, in *Hugh of St.-Victor on the Sacraments of the Christian Faith*, trans. R. J. Deferrari (Cambridge, Mass.: Mediaeval Academy, 1951).

The sanctuary at St Paul in Pensacola, Florida appropriately orders the altar, ambo, priest's chair, and the tabernacle in harmonious relationship to each other.

The Sanctuary

We now move up to the sanctuary, the part of the church where the altar is located as the central focus of the church. If the nave can be said to be the "body" or the "torso" of the church, the sanctuary is understood in this metaphor as the "head". The head governs the body, and so as Christ governs the Church we can think of the sanctuary as the place that orders and governs the rest of the church building. This symbolic importance can be seen expressed in four main ways: first, by the altar and the association of the altar with Christ; second, by the ambo (or pulpit) whence the Gospel is proclaimed; third, by the priest's place at the altar and the chair as signifying Christ's actions in the liturgical assembly; and fourth, by the traditional placement of the tabernacle in the sanctuary as signifying Christ's enduring presence in the Eucharist.

Continuing to think about the imagery where the vestibule is considered the unredeemed world, and the nave the redeemed world, the sanctuary is considered as heaven itself: it is here in the sanctuary that the Christ's perpetual sacrifice for the salvation of the world is liturgically made present for the sanctification of the entire Body. The sanctuary is in this sense the *presbyterium*, the place of the priests, which is one of the ancient terms for the sanctuary to signify that it is the place of Christ acting as High Priest in the liturgy.

One of the insights of the twentieth century Liturgical Movement was the recovery of role of the laity in the Mass as offering the sacrifice of their baptismal priesthood. This insight, however, has raised questions regarding the essential relationship between the nave and the sanctuary. Some have argued that there should be no differentiation between the nave and the sanctuary, that the priest and people are co-equals in the liturgy, and the any sense of separation (such as the altar rail) should be removed.

Lumen Gentium teaches us that there are two priesthoods, that of the clergy and that of the laity, that these are interrelated, and "each of them in its own special way is a participation in the one priesthood of Christ."[12] From this we understand the need for differentiation between the nave and the sanctuary, just as there is a differentiation between the head and the torso. There may well be a sense of tension in this understanding, and this is a theological and liturgical problem as much as an architectural one: the Body of Christ is one, yet made of many parts. The liturgy is a foretaste and participation in the heavenly liturgy, the Wedding Feast of the Lamb (especially as revealed through the symbol structure in St

---

[12] *Lumen Gentium*, 10.

John's Apocalypse), yet we are still in the here and now, in the redeemed world yet not in heaven. The sanctuary gives us a foretaste of heaven, and the liturgy gives us a foretaste and a sacramental participation in the heavenly liturgy, so the sense of organic differentiation yet integral connectedness between the nave and the sanctuary seems to be still the proper architectural and liturgical expression.

The Altar

Continuing our tour, right in the centre of the sanctuary you should see a large stone table - the altar of sacrifice. The altar is rightly considered the central focus of the church: it is not only the central focus of the Mass, the locus of the liturgical action, but it is the very reason that a church is built. The church is not just a building to contain, among other things, an altar. Rather, the altar of the Lord's sacrifice is considered, "the sign of Christ himself, the place at which the saving mysteries are carried out, and the centre of the assembly, to which the greatest reverence is due".[13] Such is the importance of the altar that it is expressly forbidden "both by custom and liturgical law to dedicate a church without dedicating the altar, for the dedication of the altar is the principal part of the whole rite".[14]

In the primitive Church altars were perhaps wood and moveable; frankly there is little archaeological or textual evidence to say anything definitive about this. Edmund Bishop's intuition about the ancient Christian altar in the first four Christian centuries seems plausible:

[13] Sacred Congregation of Rites, *Eucharisticum mysterium* (May 25, 1967), no. 24. [= EM].

[14] Sacred Congregation for the Sacraments and Divine Worship. *Dedication of a Church and an Altar*, 29th May 1977, III.I [=DOCA].

the distinguishing feature of the altar then… - whether the matter material be stone or wood, whether the altar be solid or whether it be hollow - is the prominence and respect given to the holy *Table*, as the place of sacrifice. It was in form not oblong as now in the West, but a cube: and stood as a table in the utmost simplicity. The Lord's board was too holy (too "awful" is another view) to bear anything else but the Mystic oblation itself, and such objects, the cup, the paten, the linen cloth, as were necessary for the offering up of the sacrifice.[15]

That was all: a table for the sacrifice, perhaps surmounted by a canopy, as a place of immense importance for the Christians at prayer. Nothing casual about it; nothing undignified or commonplace but protected by the "discipline of the secrets" that the ancient Church practised against profanation. Yet from the early Church we already see an association of the altar with Christ himself, with Jesus first intimating this connection, saying,

You who say, "If a man swears by the altar it has no force, but if a man swears by the offering that is on the altar, he is bound." You blind men! For which is of greater worth, the offering or the altar that makes the offering sacred? Therefore, when a man swears by the

---

[15] Edmund Bishop, *On the History of the Christian Altar* (Downside: St. Gregory Society, 1905), p. 5; reprinted in *Liturgica Historica* (Oxford: OUP, 1918), p.21.

altar he is swearing by that and by everything on it. And when a man swears by the Temple he is swearing by that and by the One who dwells in it. And when a man swears by heaven he is swearing by the throne of God and by the One who is seated there. (*Mt* 23:18-22)

This is one of those dense and complex passages that we often glance at and overlook. Christ is in fact drawing parallels between the altar and the temple and heaven itself. This association of Christ and the altar is an extension of a whole matrix of interwoven ideas about the New Covenant perfecting the Old Covenant. In the Jewish temple liturgy the priest, the altar, the place of sacrifice, and the gifts to be sacrificed were four distinct things; in Christ they are all one: Christ is the high Priest (*Heb* 4:14-15); he is the Lamb of God, the paschal sacrifice (*1 Co* 5:7; *1 P* 1:19); and Christ is the temple (*Jn* 2:21). Here Christ is telling us that he is the altar as well, the one who makes the gift sacred, and in fact is the gift on the altar, the lamb offered, the Body and Blood.

This association is why we as Catholics reverence the altar: whereas we genuflect toward the tabernacle to acknowledge the Real Presence of Christ in the Eucharist, we still properly bow to the altar. The *Rite of Dedication of the Altar*, which indicates the proper treatment that the Church gives a new altar intended to be the place of the Eucharistic sacrifice in a new church, is all expressive of this notion that the altar is directly likened to the body of the Lord. The altar is preferably to be of stone, and indeed natural stone, since Christ identified himself with "the stone which the builders rejected that has become the cornerstone." The top of the altar (the *mensa*) is to be inscribed with five crosses, one at each corner and one in the middle, to represent the Five Wounds of Christ, and these are places that are anointed with chrism by the bishop.[16] In the Rite, the altar is prepared in an analogous way to Christ's body prepared for burial: first anointed with chrism, then washed, then wrapped in linen. It is by the same logic that each year at the Paschal Triduum, the altar is stripped and left bare until Easter, representing Christ in the tomb.

Thus, when we approach the altar, we understand it not as merely a table for the sacred meal, though it is that, nor as merely the focus of the Eucharistic action at Mass, though it is that too, but truly representative of Christ himself, since Christ is both the gift and "the one who makes the gift sacred".

---

[16] DOCA, chap. 4, no. 49; also Durand, *Rationale*, bk. 1, chap. 7, nos. 29-32.

The ambo at the Cathedral in Pisa, by Giovanni Pisano, c. 1310;
reconstructed in 1926.

The Ambo

To one side or the other of the altar you should see a large reading desk for the proclamation of the Gospel. Pope St John Paul II wrote of "the two tables of the Lord" - the Table of the Word of God and the Table of the Bread of the Lord - at both of which the Church feeds her children. So this *ambo*, or *pulpit*, can be understood as a sort of a table, and the late Pope was calling us to think of this to draw the close and necessary relationship between the Liturgy of the Word and the Liturgy of the Eucharist, which "are so closely connected with each other that they form but one single act of worship".[17]

The ambo ought to be a prominent and highly visible place for the proclamation of the Gospel. This is of course a practical and architectural consideration so that everyone in the congregation can hear and see the speaker, but it also alludes to the meaning of "ambo". *Ambo* is derived from the Greek word *anabainein*, meaning "to mount to a high place". The Christian use of the idea may have been inspired by the references to such a form in the Old Testament[18] and was certainly taken from the contemporaneous Jewish

---

[17] SC, no. 56; GIRM (2010), no. 28.

[18] Cf. Neh 8:3 and the apocryphal 3 Esdras 9:42.

synagogue, which had a similar place for reading to the congregation.

Later, during the late Middle Ages and throughout the Renaissance, when preaching and the proclamation of the Word became more strongly emphasised, the ambo turned into more of a pulpit. Whereas the ambo is a free-standing structure, pulpits are usually either engaged to a column or a side wall, or integrated into the wall as a sort of a balcony.

The ambo fell into disuse for several hundred years. Even as late as the 1930s, books on church architecture often omitted the ambo entirely from consideration, but over the twentieth century some liturgists called for it to be revived as the proper place of proclamation, to give emphasis to the Liturgy of the Word, and to unite the congregation more closely to the Mass.[19] Curiously, the ambo was only cautiously introduced in the reforms of the Second Vatican Council - the conciliar documents themselves make no mention of the ambo, pulpit, or lectern, and the first directives for carrying out the liturgical reforms of the Council, *Inter Oecumenici*, merely mention in passing that "There should be a lectern or lecterns for the proclamation of the readings, so arranged that the

---

[19] Cf. Collins, Harold E., *The Church Edifice and Its Appointments*, 2nd Ed. (Westminster MD: Newman Press 1953); O'Connell, J. *Church Building & Furnishing*, London: Burns & Oates 1955): 77-78.

faithful may readily see and hear the minister."[20] This was fleshed out a few years later in the *General Instruction of the Roman Missal*, which notes: "The dignity of the word of God requires a church to have a place that is suitable for proclamation of the word and is a natural focal point for the people during the liturgy of the word."[21] Since the ambo represents the proclamation of Christ's Gospel, it ought to be a permanent, prominent, stable, and reserved place in the church.

Often today the modern ambo is designed in some derivative relationship to the altar, to draw out the connection between the "two tables", but it need not be so. The ambo regardless should be harmonious with the other sanctuary furnishings, and dignified and prominent in its own right. Above all, it should be permanent because it represents Christ's presence in the Word "which stands forever."[22]

---

[20] Sacred Congregation of Rites, *Inter Oecumenici*, 26th Sept 1964, no. 96.

[21] GIRM (1975): 272.

[22] DV, no. 26; citing Is 40:8 and *1 Pt* 1:23-25.

The Chair

Before the reforms of Vatican Council II, the priest sometimes barely sat during the entire liturgy. Churches had a simple seating bench on the side of the sanctuary for the priest, deacon, and other ministers to sit, sometimes a moveable bench, commonly called a *sedilia*. Only the cathedral had a special place of seating, in this case for the bishop on a *cathedra*. In fact, the cathedral draws its name from the seat of the bishop, the *cathedra*, and the *cathedra* is the oldest symbol of the episcopacy, predating the mitre and the crozier by centuries.

Reference is made to the apostles setting up episcopal chairs in the dioceses they founded. Both Antioch and Rome still commemorate the Feast of the Chair of Peter, as he was the founding bishop of each diocese. The symbol of the chair was taken from the *cathedra* of the Hellenic schools of philosophy and thus is primarily a symbol of the episcopal teaching office. Hence the bishop would teach from the *cathedra*, which was often elevated on a small platform, such as is found at Dura-Europos.[23] That said, there are also obvious references to the judge's seat found

---

[23] Milburn, *Early Christian Art and Architecture*, Aldershot: Scolar Press, 1988, p. 10.

in the Roman basilica and even to the king's throne, which speak to the fact that the bishop rules in the diocese.[24] The multivalent expression of the chair refers ultimately to Christ, who is ruler, judge, and teacher.

Since the Second Vatican Council, the place of the priest as the presider (lit., *the one who sits first*) has been emphasised, perhaps to draw a clearer distinction between the ministerial priesthood and the priesthood of the baptised. Since then the priest's chair has been given a strong sense of prominence in the sanctuary.

---

[24] Rykwert, *Church Building*, pp. 13 and 19; Bouyer, *Liturgy and Architecture*, p. 43.

The Crucifix

If the altar is the central focus of the liturgy and the whole church itself, the crucifix is the central *icon* of the liturgy since it is the central icon of the Faith. Together the altar and the crucifix work in conjunction to draw together the intertwined imagery of the Mass as a sacred meal, the Lord's Supper, the Passion, death and resurrection, and the Wedding Feast of the Lamb. The image of the Crucified is integrally related to the Mass, and directly symbolises the whole meaning of the Mass. It calls to mind the various facets of the Lord's act of sacrifice - becoming man and taking the form of a slave (cf. *Ph* 2:7), taking away the sins of the world (cf. *Jn* 1:29), his Passion and death - and further serves to remind the faithful of their obligation to share in Christ's suffering. It also calls to mind the resurrection, as well as the Parousia, and with it our personal triumph over death (cf. *Ep* 5:14).[25] Given these understandings, the connection between the cross and the Mass cannot be overstated.[26]

While some liturgical writers contend that the early Christians avoided the image of the crucifix because of

---

[25] Ratzinger, *Feast*, p. 143.

[26] Bouyer, *Liturgy and Architecture*, p. 117.

its association with pagan torture and humiliation, there is sufficient literary and archaeological evidence to suggest otherwise.[27] From the earliest days of Christianity, the cross was seen as central to the Faith: St Paul preached "Jesus as the crucified Christ" (*1 Co* 2:2). Paul also rather harshly reminded the people of Galatia that they were people who had had "a plain explanation...of the crucifixion of Jesus Christ" (*Ga* 3:1).

While the records of the early Church describe the Mass as a participation in the sacrifice of Christ , the liturgical use of the crucifix to signify this is a much later development. At first it seems a simple cross was painted on the east wall of the apse, first as a sign of the Parousia, and later as a sign of the Passion. Probably from the seventh century we begin to see processional crosses, and the image of the cross used liturgically. When the Church began to use the image of the Crucified to express artistically the meaning of the Mass, from the seventh to the twelfth century, Christ was nearly always shown alive, often dressed in finery with a jewelled crown, reigning from the cross. The clear message in the Byzantine and Romanesque ages was of Christ in majesty, and the most common depictions are of Jesus surrounded by a body halo, expressive of his reigning in heaven. Toward the end of the Romanesque era, particularly in Spain, we begin to see increasingly more

---

[27] O'Connell, *Church Building*, p. 101.

realistic crucifixes, especially as the art of polychromed wood sculpture developed. Still Christ was often depicted more frequently alive than dead, looking serenely or even with compassion from the cross, expressing his triumph over death.

From the mid-thirteenth century, we see a profusion of images of Christ naked and dead on the cross. This convention is arguably an artistic response to the theological development of the doctrine of transubstantiation, the assertion that the Eucharist was indeed the Body of Christ, which becomes expressed during this time with the increased devotion to *Corpus Christi*. The historicity and physical reality of Christ's death and resurrection become the central referent of the Eucharistic celebration, and so in consequence the crucifix becomes an important liturgical referent in the church. Rood screens above the entrance into the sanctuary, with Christ shown crucified between flanking statues of his mother and St John, called to mind the Gospel event as an aid to the piety of the faithful. These became increasingly more realistic, particularly in the Renaissance as human anatomy once again became an area of study for artists, and in the Baroque age crucifixion scenes become increasingly more spectacular and ostentatious.

Since the time of Trent, and particularly in the liturgical reforms of St Charles Borromeo, the crucifix has been made the central icon of the liturgy. This was undoubtedly in response to the challenges of the Reformation that denied the Real Presence and the Sacrifice of the Mass.

So when we see the crucifix in a church, and particularly at Mass, it is a deliberate reminder to us of Christ's saving actions in his Passion, death and resurrection. The Church has long been opposed to "Resurrection Crosses" which show no trace of Christ's suffering. The only appropriate image for the liturgy is to be "a cross, with the figure of Christ crucified upon it, either on the altar or near it, where it is clearly visible to the assembled congregation. It is appropriate that such a cross, which calls to mind for the faithful the saving Passion of the Lord, remain near the altar even outside of liturgical celebrations."[28] Thus it is that as we participate at Mass, we are called to fulfil the words of the prophet Zechariah, recounted at the Crucifixion of the Lord: "They will look on the one whom they have pierced (*Jn* 19:37).

---

[28] GIRM (2010), no. 308.

The tabernacle at Our Savior Catholic Center is located in the main apse to provide a quite place for prayer, while directly connected to the nave and sanctuary.

The Tabernacle

The last item we will consider in our church tour is the tabernacle, a sort of strongbox usually located directly behind the altar, in which is reserved the Blessed Sacrament. I say "usually" because over the past fifty years the tabernacle has been experimentally moved around the church, sometimes on the high altar, sometimes to one side of the sanctuary, sometimes in a sort of cabinet like the case that holds the Jewish Torah, sometimes in an entirely separate chapel. There are a number of liturgical laws governing the proper placement of the tabernacle, but to properly understand the reasoning behind the liturgical laws, it is best first to understand the symbolic language of the tabernacle.

The modern Catholic tabernacle finds its origin in the Tent of Dwelling which the Lord instructed Moses to build in the desert: "Build me a sanctuary so that I may dwell among them. In making the tabernacle and its furnishings you must follow exactly the pattern I shall show you." (*Ex* 25:8-9). In the Exodus account, before the Tent of Dwelling was constructed, the Israelites sinned against the Lord by worshipping the Gold Calf (*Ex* 32). Moses thus set up another tent outside the camp, the "tent of meeting"

(*Ex* 33:7-11), where the Lord would appear as the pillar of cloud. After Moses restored the Israelites to the Lord, he then set out to have them construct this Tent of Dwelling (*Ex* 35-39). The idea of the tabernacle then is both a place of meeting and a place of dwelling; indeed, *tabernaculum* means a little tent, which in primitive cultures was a place of civilisation, socialisation, protection, and culture apart from the hostile environment of raw nature. So as we approach the tabernacle in the church we should see it as a place of meeting with our Lord, where Christ is always present to be with us in our midst, as the Lord was present among the people of Israel.

The Lord gave very explicit instructions, the first architectural specifications, for how the tent was to be built, and how the various liturgical items were to be crafted. The primary purpose of the tent was to house the Ark of the Covenant, a large gold-covered and gold-lined casket to keep the tablets of the Covenant within, with two sculpted angels facing each other. On top of the Ark was a "mercy seat" (*Kapporeth*) where the Lord would manifest himself in the form of the *Shekinah* (the "glory of the Lord"): "There I will meet you and there, from above the cover, between the two cherubim on the ark of the covenant, I will tell you all that I command you regarding the Israelites" (*Ex* 25:22). There were numerous other elements found in the Tabernacle - a table for the showbread, a menorah, an altar of incense, and a veil separating the tent into two chambers: the "Holy" for the lamp, table and altar, and the "Holy of Holies" for the Ark alone.

In this arrangement we see all the basic symbolic elements of our encounter with God, which continues to this day in the Catholic Mass. The Venerable Bede in the early eighth century compiled a general patristic interpretation of this, showing the complex allegorical meaning of the tabernacle in relation to the Church. The "showbread" is a prefiguration of the Eucharist, baked from "the finest wheat" into twelve loaves (representing the twelve tribes and later the twelve apostles), and renewed each week at the Sabbath when Aaron and his sons (that is, the High Priest and the lay priesthood) might eat of them. The menorah designates the Church universal, which shows the path of light to all. It is illuminated by seven lamps, the seven gifts of the Holy Spirit, but also the six days of creation and the seventh day of rest, thus expressing the perfection of all things given by God. This menorah is still symbolically represented in the Catholic Mass of the Pope or another bishop, where seven candles are placed on the altar. It is interesting that liturgical items (table, altar, lamps) are kept in a separate chamber from the Ark. Bede explains this according to the tradition of the Church Fathers, as follows: the "Holy" represents the redeemed world, in which the Church serves to feed the faithful from the table of bread, to illuminate the world with the Gospel, and to offer sacrifice at the altar - but "the

Church does not yet deserve to be admitted to the vision of the Redeemer in heaven".[29] The final consummation of the Lamb and the Bride has not yet occurred, that will happen in the future, and the unity of all things anticipated in Revelation chapters 21 and 22 will then be understood. This final consummation is a recovery of the original unity of the Garden which we mentioned earlier.

So in Christ we also see the establishment of a new unity between the presence of God in the *Shekinah* and the liturgy of the Church: the veil that separated the two realities is the veil that was torn asunder at the death of Christ: "But Jesus, again crying out in a loud voice, yielded up his spirit. At that, the veil of the Temple was torn in two from top to bottom" (*Mt* 27: 50-51).

Thus we live in this in-between state, where Christ has pierced the veil of separation and united himself to us all, both priest and people, through the liturgy in the sacrifice of the altar and the Bread of Life and the Gospel, and yet we still await the final consummation which the Mass anticipates. So a lot is going on in the symbol of the tabernacle in the sanctuary. The Lord is present, yet his Body and Blood are still veiled under the appearance of bread and wine, and the Body of Christ is itself veiled in the tabernacle, which is a place separate from the rest of the sanctuary and from the rest of the church. This theme

---

[29]Bede, *On the Tabernacle*, Book 1, 8. Cf. Holder, Arthur. *Bede: On the Tabernacle*. Liverpool: Liverpool University Press, 1994.

of veiling and separation has reverberated throughout this exploration of the church architecture, thinking about the *disciplina arcana* when only the baptised could attend Mass, or the doors and gates that mark the church off from the secular world, and the baptistery as an expression of reclaiming our inheritance of the Garden.

All of these aspects are part of the Church's considerations for the form and artistic expression of the tabernacle. The liturgical laws regarding the tabernacle itself are simple and straightforward. There is to be one and only one tabernacle in a church or oratory for permanent and regular reservation, and this tabernacle is to be constructed so it is solid, opaque, unbreakable, fireproof, and inviolable.[30] In keeping with the ancient custom of showing highest respect, a veil (*conopaeum*) should completely cover the tabernacle, recalling the veil that covered the Ark of the Covenant.[31] "A lamp must burn perpetually before it, as a sign of the honour paid to the Lord",[32] and this lamp announces Christ's presence. While in the ancient Church there were many different ways of reserving the Eucharist, from the twelfth century the

---

[30] EM, no. 52; GIRM (2010), no. 314; ID, no. 25; Johnson, *Planning for Liturgy*, p. 35.

[31] O'Connell, *Church Building*, p. 172; Ex 40; also ID, no. 25. This is not necessary if the tabernacle has artistic merit.

[32] ID, no. 25. This seems to clarify EM, no. 57, by replacing "should" with "must." Also, GIRM (2010), no. 316.

tabernacle became the preferred, dominant, and finally legislated method of safekeeping the Blessed Sacrament.

Since the Second Vatican Council there has been some confusion regarding the placement and expression of the tabernacle. Some liturgists argued that the tabernacle should not be in the sanctuary, claiming it competed for attention with the altar. Others allowed it in the sanctuary as long as it was obscured by a screen during the Mass. Some claimed that Eucharistic adoration is essentially a private and personal devotion, which somehow conflicted with the public nature of the Eucharistic celebration at Mass. Yet others insisted that the altar was the main focus of the liturgy, and that nothing should compete with it for attention. Whatever our views on these questions, nevertheless it is the Church's clear desire that the tabernacle ought to be in placed in a position that "is truly noble, prominent, conspicuous, worthily decorated, and suitable for prayer".

There should be no real theological grounds for confusion between the reserved Body of Christ, and how Christ comes to us in the Eucharistic celebration. The one occurs in space and time as we participate in the Mass, the other is the continued real presence of Christ in the Eucharist by virtue of that liturgical action. These are but two aspects on one spiritual and sacramental reality: that Christ continues to dwell among his people. The Church commonly uses the exact same language of Eucharist quite indiscriminately to speak of both the Holy Mass and the reserved Sacred Species as the centre of the Church. In *Eucharisticum mysterium* it is said that "the celebration of the Eucharist is the true center of the whole Christian life."[33] On the other hand, Pope Paul VI, in *The Credo of the People of God*, calls the tabernacle "the living heart of our churches".[34] The Eucharist reserved and the Eucharistic action are both "centres" because they are but two facets of the same thing. As such, there is no division; recall St Paul's admonishment, "Has Christ been parcelled out?" (*1 Co* 1:13) With this in mind, Pope Benedict XVI's *Sacramentum Caritatis* commends that, "The correct positioning of the tabernacle contributes to the recognition of Christ's real presence in the Blessed Sacrament. Therefore, the place where the Eucharistic species are reserved, marked by a sanctuary lamp, should be readily visible to everyone entering the church."[35]

But to the question of the placement of the tabernacle, its intrinsic meaning and architectural and canonical requirements should if properly understood prevent any appearance of conflict with anything else going on in the sanctuary, if indeed it is placed there. The tabernacle is already necessarily distinct and separate from the altar by virtue of its construction: it is properly opaque and solid, and even to be veiled with a *conopaeum* if the container

---

[33] EM, no. 6.

[34] Paul VI, *The Credo of the People of God* (June 30, 1968).

[35] Benedict XVI, *Sacramentum Caritatis*, no. 69.

itself has no distinct architectural merit. In short, the tabernacle itself is already a liturgical distinct place: it is a small chapel, a room unto itself, as was the Tent of Dwelling in the Courtyard of the Priests and the Holy of Holies in the Tent and Temple. The tabernacle is simply a device for "veiling the *Shekinah*". This is why tabernacles cannot be made transparent; when the Church displays the Body of Christ for public adoration, a monstrance is used for that and for Benediction. But a tabernacle is not a monstrance; this seems to be a mistake made both by the modern liturgist who thinks a tabernacle in the sanctuary "distracting", as well as by the pious traditionalist priest who does not want to celebrate Mass *versus populum* since he would be "turning his back on the Lord." Both treat the tabernacle as if it were a monstrance and both fail to differentiate between the unveiled "Glory of the Lord" (the *Shekinah*) and the veiling that the "tent" provides. Rather, having the tabernacle in the sanctuary can help us understand the presence of Lord among his people.

So when we enter a church, we properly greet the Lord in the tabernacle. We should be able to readily see the tabernacle from the nave, and we should know the Lord is present in the tabernacle by the lighted sanctuary lamp. We are encouraged to visit the Blessed Sacrament at times apart from the Mass, as it is always appropriate to come before the Lord with our concerns and prayers, to keep company with Christ and grow in our relationship with him.

Church Architecture and "Active Participation"

The overarching theme of this book is on how the Church calls for churches to be designed and built with deliberate intention. The purpose of a church is to be a place set aside for the worship of God, and this building is intended to both express and facilitate the Church's understanding of how we are called to participate sacramentally in liturgy and the spiritual life. As such, over time the Church has developed a rich and complex language of signs, symbols, and sacraments, of liturgical expressions, architectural forms, styles and arrangements, sacred art and iconography, in order to communicate the things of God. It has been just over a century since Pope St Pius X called for us to be concerned with the sanctity and dignity of the church building, namely because this is the place that each week Christ's faithful assemble to grow in holiness through their active participation in the weekly Mass. That past century witnessed a significant change in the way Catholics build their churches, so now alongside grand, formal, traditionally styled, and civically scaled buildings we see buildings serving as churches that are sometimes idiosyncratic or plain uninteresting.

The careful planning of the church allows each person to take one's rightful place in the liturgy, focusing on the sanctuary, to encourage a proper sense of active participation.

Yet as has been hopefully made clear, the function of these buildings is not merely to provide a "skin for the liturgical action". Rather, the function of a church building is to accommodate both the body and the soul, the local community and the Church Universal, the past memory and tradition as well as some foretaste of the future glory. The Church rightly invites our church buildings to be "signs and symbols of the heavenly realities", and the building itself is intended to be an aid to us as we engage in the Sacred Liturgy in the fulness of our humanity.

Catholicism promotes beautiful art because it engages us in our senses; sights and sounds and smells and textures and body postures all contribute to this engagement. Beauty and grandeur lift the heart; orderly and rational and well-proportioned churches please the mind; carefully developed and orthodox iconography informs the intellect and direct us to the things of God; and dignified sacred music allows us to join with the angels and the saints in the heavenly praises. An atmosphere of dignity at Mass gives us the psychological space to contemplate, to still our hearts and minds, to hear the voice of Jesus, to bring our needs to the Lord, and to focus on our need to grow ever closer to Christ through our own personal sacrifice of praise along with the gifts offered at the altar.

The Church is quite deliberate about this approach to her architecture because she earnestly desires that we, "when present at this mystery of faith, should not be there as strangers or silent spectators; on the contrary, through a good understanding of the rites and prayers [we] should take part in the sacred action conscious of what [we] are doing, with devotion and full collaboration."[36] This is the heart of the active participation Pope St Pius X called for. His successor, Pope Pius XII, noted that "the worship rendered by the Church to God must be, in its entirety, interior as well as exterior." Worship is primarily an internal disposition, but the nature of man as body and soul requires an appropriate exterior expression.

We live in the world of materiality and engage in all things through our senses: to deny this is to deny our very humanity and God's plan that we should come to him through the sacraments. Rather, we should consider the whole church building to be a sacramental assistance in our participation in the liturgy. We are not behaviourists - environment and conditioning do not determine us - but a church building as a whole and the various parts of it should all work harmoniously and be conducive to our prayers and our understanding of how we are called to engage in "fully conscious, and active participation" in the Holy Liturgy. If a building does this, its architect has accomplished what the Church asks.

---

[36] Vatican Council II, *Sacrosanctum Concilium*, no 48.